LITTLE BOOK OF

LINERS

LITTLE BOOK OF
LINERS

First published in the UK in 2012

© Demand Media Limited 2012

www.demand-media.co.uk

Printed and bound in China

ISBN 978-1-909217-22-5

Contents

Introduction

The great ocean liners used to be a symbol of national power and pride. For most of their history they were the largest moving objects built by man and, like the rockets launched during the space race between the United States and the Soviet Union, they represented the pinnacle of human achievement, symbols of a nation's industrial and technological prowess.

And, like the space race, there was a constant game of one-upmanship between the major ship-building nations. It almost seemed as if every new ship had to be longer, heavier and faster than its rivals. This race captured the imagination of the public, with society's elite clamouring for berths aboard the new ships.

The race for profits and prestige often ended in disaster, however. The story of the *Titanic* is well documented but other great liners like the *Andrea Doria*, *Empress of Ireland*, *Britannic*, *Lusitania* and the first *Queen Elizabeth* all foundered, some in mysterious circumstances. Indeed, the sinking of the *Titanic* was such a newsworthy event that it has often been associated with the decline of the British Empire.

During the First World War, some of these great ships were used as troop transports or hospital ships, but, this being a time of total war, they were often targeted by the enemy. After the conflict, the roaring twenties brought renewed interest in the liners, and they

somehow survived the Great Depression.

After the Second World War, the liners enjoyed another renaissance, but by the 1970s they were beginning to feel outdated, and the increasing popularity of air travel seemed to herald the beginning of the end. People wanted to cut their travel time so they could get to work, not enjoy making the journey by sea because it cut into profits. The oil crisis brought home the cost of running a fleet of great ships and interest in the glory of the trans-Atlantic run gradually faded. Today, a new fleet of cruise ships rules the waves, and there is only one true liner left in service. Maybe one day they'll make a comeback...

Above: The *Andrea Doria* lies mortally wounded after a collision with the Stockholm in 1956.

Right: *RMS Titanic* leaving Belfast to start her sea trials shortly before her disastrous maiden voyage of April 1912.

The Age of Steam

In the Middle Ages, ships had two purposes: they were warships bristling with guns and carrying men and equipment, or they were merchant vessels plying the trade routes. The Royal Navy was the dominant military power throughout the 18th century and its ships policed the world's oceans so that it could keep the peace among the colonies. Keeping in contact with the empire was dependant on the speed and seaworthiness of the ships of the time, however. Most were timber-hulled and powered by sail and they were frequently at the mercy of wind and wave. A round trip to Australia, for example, could take up to eight months. And any passengers onboard were viewed merely as cargo, their passage seen only as a way of making the route profitable for the owners.

This changed with the invention of the piston-driven steam engine in the late 18th century and the opening of the Suez Canal in 1869. The latter shortened sailing time to the Far East by several weeks, while the former was soon being installed in the ships of the time (although an Atlantic crossing was still beyond their modest capabilities). In 1819 however, a converted American ship, the *Savannah*, arrived in Britain after a month at sea. Although most of the Atlantic crossing was made under sail power, it triggered interest in these steamships and a new age dawned.

In 1829, the steam-powered *Sophia Jane* paddled halfway around the world from London to Sydney. This was just the beginning for the steamers. The great leap in maritime history was continued by Arthur Anderson and Brodie Wilcox (founders of P&O) in 1837 when they pioneered a mail service between England and the Iberian Peninsula. Three years later, great rival Samuel Cunard launched a trans-Atlantic mail service with his ship *Britannia*. Passengers were also allowed onboard so that the route could become profitable, and their numbers grew with each safe passage.

In the following years, steam power became a serious threat to sail. But the ships were small and demand exceeded the small number of berths available. All this was about to change. British engineer Isambard Kingdom Brunel was the visionary who came up with the idea

Above: A painting of Samuel Cunard's mail ship *Britannia*.

LITTLE BOOK OF **LINERS**

of building a passenger liner specifically for the trans-Atlantic route. Brunel's first ship, the *Great Western*, launched in Bristol in 1837, was still a timber-hulled vessel but she was one of the largest ships afloat and could carry 150 passengers.

Her maiden crossing of the Atlantic was not without incident, however. A fire broke out in the engine room before she'd even reached open water and Brunel was injured in the confusion. A number of passengers promptly cancelled their trip and only seven were aboard when she finally left Avonmouth. Sensing the opportunity to trump their rivals, the American ship *Sirius* was coaxed into service and, with a four-day head-start, she comfortably beat the *Great Western* to New York. But the latter's crossing had been much smoother, she still had plenty of coal in her bunkers and she arrived only one day behind. The ship eventually crossed the Atlantic 45 times before she was sold.

Brunel's second ship, the *Great Britain*, revolutionised travel and ushered in the era of the ocean liner. At 322 feet (98 metres) long and 3,600 tonnes, she was 70 feet (20m) longer and almost twice the size of her predecessor. He fitted a steam engine and screw propeller in an iron-hulled ship for the first time. She made more than 30 round trips to Australia (including taking the first English cricket tourists in 1861) and proved that transporting up to 360 paying passengers in comfort and safety could turn a profit. (Although the ship carried thousands of immigrants to Australia, she was eventually retired to the Falkland Islands in 1884 before being scuttled in 1937. In 1970 the ship was saved and returned to Bristol where she now attracts more than 150,000 visitors each year.)

In 1854 Brunel upped the ante for all other shipbuilders by laying down the keel of the *Great Eastern* on the banks of the Thames. The ship was a leviathan: at 692 feet (211 metres) and 19,000 tonnes, she was six times larger than anything else afloat (and would remain the largest ship in the world for nearly 50 years). She would be capable of steaming to Australia in half the time of the fastest sailing ships and would not need to stop to take on more coal. She was designed to carry 4,000 passengers or up to 10,000 troops.

The ship was not the great success Brunel envisioned, however. She was beset with financial problems and never

made a trip to Australia. She was sold instead to compete on the Atlantic run but the smaller ships were financially secure and offered a similar service so she ran at a huge loss and had to be sold again. A series of accidents saw her taken out of passenger service to lay submarine cables across the Atlantic instead. She ended up being used as a giant advertising hoarding in Liverpool, an ignominious end for such a magnificent feat of engineering. Thankfully, Brunel didn't live to see the ship's demise – he died in 1859 – but his dream of steamships circling the globe

Above: The hybrid steam-sail ship *SS Savannah*.

certainly became a reality in the years after his death.

Although travelling by steamship in the late 19th century may have a ring of romance about it, the reality was somewhat different. Spending weeks at sea with no air-conditioning or refrigeration, and being tossed about in heavy seas with acrid smoke belching from funnels while animals were slaughtered for food below-decks wouldn't win any awards today.

With the opening of the Suez Canal, the British immediately feared their dominance of the waves would be threatened by the French because they would then have access to the riches of the Orient. They solved the problem by investing in the canal in 1876 and securing the vital trade and mail route. The journey to the jewel in Britain's imperial crown, India, by sail around the Cape of Good Hope took two months, but this had been reduced to a couple of weeks by steamship through the canal. This was obviously extremely good for business as more trips could be made each year.

The French and Americans didn't want Britain to have everything its own way, however. They also built steamships that could compete on the same routes: the race for profits and prestige had begun. Sail gradually gave way to hybrid ships with steam engines before the latter took over completely. The number of funnels a ship had rather than the number of masts now symbolised its power. The North Atlantic run was seen as the most important so the competing nations vied for supremacy, with the shortest time taken to complete the crossing giving the parent line and its country bragging rights. Another new age had dawned.

Left: The mighty *Great Eastern* is beached before being broken up.

GREAT EASTERN

Cunard, White Star
& the Germans

When the British started operating a monthly mail service from Cornwall to New York in the late 18th century, its ships tended to carry a few passengers but no cargo. In 1818, the American Black Ball Line began a regular service back to Liverpool with its clipper ships, although they were soon overtaken by steamships that started to dominate the passenger trade. Parliament then decided that to remain competitive, the mail service run by the post office could be replaced by private shipping companies owned and run by such men as the arctic explorer Sir William Parry and a young Nova Scotian Joseph Howe, both of whom lobbied for steam service to Halifax. Howe came to Britain

in 1838 and met compatriot Samuel Cunard who, as a ship owner, was in London on business.

Cunard and Howe soon formed an alliance so the former returned to Halifax to raise capital while Howe lobbied the British government to introduce a North Atlantic service, which he claimed would be important for the military should there be any problems with the empire.

The Great Western Steamship Company, British-American and the St George Steam Packet Company all bid for the route but the admiralty blocked them because they couldn't introduce it quickly enough (their ships would need modernising if they were going to survive repeated crossings in poor

Left: Sir Samuel
Cunard.

weather). Cunard heard about the deal and bid for it even though he didn't have any ships capable of fulfilling his end of the bargain (he had the backing of the Royal Navy as well as some political clout in Canada instead).

Great Western protested that Cunard could not deliver his promise but Parry accepted his offer in 1838 (they offered a three-ship Liverpool–Halifax service that could be extended to reach Boston and/or Montreal). A fourth ship was promised which allowed them to run monthly departures from Liverpool during the winter and every two weeks throughout the rest of the year. Great

LITTLE BOOK OF **LINERS**

Right: A painting
of the original
Oceanic.

Western was so incensed that they approached parliament but, having investigated the background to the bids, the government sided with Cunard and upheld the admiralty's decision.

Cunard knew he had to deliver so he recruited more investors and together they formed the British & North American Royal Mail Steam Packet Company (B&NARMSPC) in 1840. Cunard contributed 20 percent of the funds while investor Sir George Burns oversaw the shipbuilding side of the business.

In spring the same year, the paddle steamer *Unicorn* made the company's first crossing to Halifax and then headed on to Montreal. In July, the first of the four ocean-going steamers of the new *Britannia* class liners left Liverpool, arriving in Halifax 12 days later. The ship then headed for Boston to ensure the company kept to its promise and schedule. Over the following two years the company's ships averaged 12 days for the outward and homeward legs but this needed to be improved upon if passenger numbers were to be increased, so two larger ships were ordered (one of which would have to replace the *Columbia*, which sank off Seal Island in 1843,

CUNARD, WHITE STAR & THE GERMANS

thankfully without any casualties).

By 1845, Cunard's line was carrying more passengers than the traditional sailing companies. The government upped its investment so the line could continue to flourish. Cunard put the money into four more paddle steamers and opened an alternate route that took passengers direct to New York instead of either Halifax or Boston. The traditional sailing lines were frozen out and were reduced to feeding off the scraps generated by the immigrant trade.

Cunard's ships were painted in distinctive livery that included having a red funnel with narrow black bands and a black top. (This tradition continues today on the *Queen Mary 2*.) The company's fine safety record helped it garner most of the early trade and brought it considerable success. British-American, on the other hand, foundered after its flagship, the *President*, sank in a storm. And Great Western entered choppy waters after the *Great Britain* ran aground after poor navigation. Cunard had seen off the first two challenges (it also saw off the British Inman and American Collins Lines after both suffered disasters) but it would now face a bigger threat in the shape of White Star.

The first company called White Star was founded in Liverpool by John Pilkington and Henry Wilson in the mid-18th century. It focused initially on the immigrant and working trade to Australia because there was the promise of a prosperous new life in a country where gold had just been discovered. The company didn't have enough capital to commission ships of its own so it initially chartered sailing ships like the *White Star*, *Ellen*, *Ben Nevis* and *Iowa*. They also acquired the largest ship of its time, the *Tayleur*, but it foundered on its maiden voyage at Lambay Island in the North Atlantic. This would haunt the company for years, and history sometimes repeats itself…

White Star then bought its first steamship, the *Royal Standard*, in 1863 before it merged with two smaller subsidiary lines, Black Ball and Eagle. The company now went under the rather grand name of The Liverpool, Melbourne & Oriental Steam Navigation Company Limited, but it was a poorly conceived deal and White Star was forced to pull out and devote its attention to the increasingly prosperous Liverpool to New York service. White Star initially borrowed a great deal of

money to finance its shipbuilding but, when the Royal Bank of Liverpool went under in 1867, the company couldn't pay its outstanding debt (then £527,000 but in today's money £34 million) and it was forced to declare bankruptcy.

The company was saved by The Oceanic Steam Navigation Company, which had just been formed by Thomas Ismay. Ismay had been a director of the National Line and in 1868 he saw the opportunity to buy White Star (and pay off a small amount of the bankruptcy settlement as a goodwill gesture). He then decided to commandeer a fleet to ply the North Atlantic alongside the new Cunarders.

Ismay was soon being approached by potential investors, one of whom, Gustav Schwabe, was a noted merchant whose nephew was renowned shipbuilder Gustav Wolff (of Harland & Wolff fame). The two men struck a deal whereby Schwabe would fund their new line as long as Ismay used his nephew to build their ships. Ismay saw how profitable such a partnership would be and agreed to them using Harland & Wolff, providing the yard refused to build ships for any of their rivals.

Ismay's new company, the Oceanic Steam Navigation Company, then placed its first orders the following year. This entity would now operate the steamers under construction, of which there would be six in an *Oceanic* class: *Oceanic* herself, *Baltic*, *Republic* and *Atlantic* would then be joined by the larger *Celtic* and *Adriatic*. (White Star traditionally ended its ship's names with *ic*. They also adopted a buff-coloured funnel with a black peak and the twin-tailed red pennant with five-pointed star to distinguish themselves further from rival lines.) So, having been on the brink of collapse only a few years earlier, the new White Star now had a fleet and was fully operational between Liverpool and New York (with a stop at Queenstown in southern Ireland).

The company made a disastrous start, however, when the *SS Atlantic* foundered near Nova Scotia in 1873 with the loss of 535 lives. A Canadian inquiry blamed poor navigation by an inexperienced crew, although the company was later cleared by the British Board of Trade.

White Star had the financial backing to survive this early crisis and its ships – like the *Britannic*, *Teutonic* and *Majestic* – were soon competing for the fastest Atlantic crossing. By 1899 Thomas Ismay had commissioned *Oceanic II*, one of the biggest (the first to exceed Brunel's *Great Eastern*'s dimensions) but most beautiful steamers built during the period. The ship hinted at White Star's plans for the future because the ship was built with luxury and fuel economy rather than speed as its priority. So, at a time when Cunard was building the first greyhounds of the seas, and White Star was countering them with ships of the highest class, the Germans decided they could bring something to the table: cheap, safe emigration to the United States.

LITTLE BOOK OF **LINERS**

Norddeutscher Lloyd (NDL) was founded in Bremen in 1856. The line immediately entered the market as a passenger and cargo service from its home port to New York. The *Bremen* itself was the company's flagship and it entered service the same year. Two more steamships were added to the fleet so they could operate a continuous service to Hoboken in New Jersey. The company went from strength to strength and was soon competing with the steerage accommodation on the Cunard and White Star ships, which was developing into a major share of the market. Indeed, NDL's vast fleet carried nearly a quarter of a million people to the New World in 1913. There was trouble on the horizon, however.

The outbreak of the First World War saw practically the company's entire fleet, which then numbered more than 130 ships, stranded in Hoboken. When the US entered the war in 1917, the ships were officially confiscated and their Hoboken port turned over to the American navy for the remainder of the conflict. Despite ceding many of its ships to the US and Britain at the end of the war, NDL bought the base back and resumed trading in 1922. NDL promptly launched two massive new ships, the *Bremen* and *Europa*, towards the end of the 1920s.

The Second World War was equally unpleasant for the line and it again had its fleet impounded in 1941 after the US was forced into the conflict after the Japanese attack on Pearl Harbour. The only ship to escape the clutches of the Allies was the *Bremen*, which managed to make it back across the Atlantic to Murmansk before finally docking in her home port (where she remained for the rest of the war).

NDL took longer to recover after the Second World War and didn't resume trading until 1954 with three ships purchased from the Swedish-American Line. The company also struggled to cope with the competition from the aviation industry and eventually merged with Hamburg-America in 1970.

NDL's ships had a fine reputation for safety, efficiency and value but they were also fast. The first time the line took the record for the fastest Atlantic crossing had been by the *Elbe* in 1881 (eight days). The most famous crossing was probably by the *Bremen* in 1929, which once again secured the Blue Riband for Germany.

The Blue Riband

Crossing the Atlantic in the shortest possible time soon became a matter of national pride for shipbuilders and passengers alike. Indeed, there was no greater kudos than being able to boast that your passengers had just made the crossing on the fastest ship in the world. Britain took an early lead in the bragging rights. Her liners were bigger and faster than anything the Americans or French could build and they cemented her position as the greatest maritime nation in history.

Indeed, the *Sirius* is the first ship generally credited with winning the Blue Riband (the phrase didn't come into popular usage until 1910 and was only credited for the westbound run,

so before then – and afterwards on the eastbound runs – ships were known simply as record-breakers). Brunel's *Great Western* snatched the title back the following day and it then made the first 10-knot (18.5km/h) crossing in 1843. The Cunard steamship *Asia* then raised the average speed (because most of the ships sailed different routes of varying lengths, the best average speed claims the record, not the shortest crossing time) to 12.25 knots (23km/h) in 1850.

The Americans were keen to lay down a marker, however, and the government-funded Collins Line reclaimed the record with the *Pacific* later the same year. Their elation was short-lived because the company lost

three ships and went bust in 1858. This left Cunard's last paddle-steamer *Scotia* to claim the record with a 14.5-knot (27km/h) run in 1862. With the demise of the paddle-steamer, the new ships were all single-screw express liners. The two main contenders were Cunard and the new White Star Line. The latter's *Adriatic* soon took the record but then a new contender emerged in the form of the Guion Line's *Arizona*.

Although the company was primarily involved in the cheap steerage trade, William Pearce became convinced that

Above: The *Sirius* is considered to be the first holder of the Blue Riband after its trans-Atlantic crossing in 1837.

comfort could be sacrificed for speed to shorten the crossing and increase profits. Cunard rejected his idea so he approached Guion and they accepted. Three of their ships traded the record, with the *Oregon* raising the average speed to an impressive 18.6 knots (34km/h) in 1884. Cunard immediately saw the value in cutting crossing times further and *Etruria* almost exceeded 20 knots (36km/h) before the company realised that this was probably the maximum speed achievable by a single-screw vessel.

There then followed a brief battle between the Inman Line's *City of New York* and *City of Paris*, White Star's *Teutonic* and *Majestic* and Cunard's *Campania* and *Lucania*. The latter appeared to have claimed the title for a while with a 21.8-knot (40km/h) run in 1894 but a new entrant was about to join the battle for the Blue Riband (and the profits and prestige).

Queen Victoria's grandson, Kaiser Wilhelm II, embarked on a shipbuilding programme that would see Germany challenge the British dominance of the waves. He'd been to their fleet review in 1889 and was so impressed with the Royal Navy that he became determined

Left: The Inman Lines ship *City of Paris* also made the fastest Atlantic crossing.

to exceed its power in both number of ships and their size. In 1897, the first of these liners, the *Kaiser Wilhelm der Grosse* (one of four sisters), was built with four funnels and displaced over 14,000 tonnes. She had an immediate impact on the maritime culture of the time because she took the Blue Riband for the fastest North Atlantic crossing from the British Cunard ships on her maiden voyage. Germany had arrived as a major maritime power. It was a position she

consolidated when the *Deutschland*, a Hamburg-America Line ship, snatched the record three times in the first few years of the 20th century. There were problems with these greyhounds of the seas, however. During their high-speed runs the vibrations could become so bad that they were nicknamed 'cocktail shakers'.

Cunard and White Star realised that passengers were being put off by these problems so decided to emphasise

comfort and safety over speed. Within a year, the White Star Line had commissioned the greatest shipbuilders of the time, Harland & Wolff, to build a 705-foot (214-metre) flagship, the *Oceanic* (the first ship to exceed the length of Brunel's *Great Eastern*). No expense was spared and the ship's interior was hailed as the benchmark for style and comfort for the new century. Even the German Kaiser was impressed with her fittings and

fixtures. Despite another new White Star ship, the *Celtic*, being launched in 1901, both the British vessels had been built for comfort and not speed so the Blue Riband stayed in Germany.

After Queen Victoria's death in 1901, Kaiser Wilhelm devoted his energy into building a navy and merchant fleet that could also challenge the British. His uncle, Britain's new King Edward, was uneasy with this new phase of German expansion but there was soon another

Above: In 1872 White Star's *Adriatic* became the first screw-driven liner to claim the prestigious Blue Riband, although the phrase didn't come into use until 1910.

potential enemy on the horizon: railroad tycoon JP Morgan's money. He bought the White Star Line, which meant the British could no longer commandeer its vessels in times of war. Morgan then approached Cunard with an even bolder offer.

Cunard was left with no alternative but to lobby the British government for support. The government not only prevented the takeover but bankrolled the building of Cunard's next two ships, which, to snub Morgan, were to be the finest ever launched, the so-called super-liners *Mauretania* and *Lusitania*. At nearly 800 feet (240 metres) long and 32,000 tonnes, and powered by direct-action Parsons steam engines delivering 70,000 horsepower, they were built for peace but designed to be converted into troop transports in times of war. This was a measure of how seriously the British took the German threat, not only from their ships on the trans-Atlantic route, but also from the imperial ambitions.

The *Mauretania* promptly regained the Blue Riband for Britain with an eastbound crossing at an average speed of 24 knots (44km/h). Two years later she recaptured the westbound speed record with a run that would remain unchallenged for 20 years. Although the government stipulated that it would commandeer the ships as auxiliary transports in wartime, Cunard was far more concerned with making the route profitable. This was an era of emigration from Europe to the New World and vast third-class compartments were crammed with the poor seeking new lives in the land of plenty. There was no shortage of takers for the higher classes of accommodation either – it was seen as a sign of wealth and social standing to travel first class on the new Cunarders. Indeed, the company soon captured the majority of the immigrant trade with its fast, safe ships.

British ships and the industry behind them was once again the envy of the world. They had taken on the Germans and won. But Cunard didn't have it all its own way. Bruce Ismay, chairman of the White Star Line, couldn't help wanting a piece of the trans-Atlantic action so he approached JP Morgan for financial backing and commissioned three magnificent new *Olympic*-class ships: *Olympic*, *Gigantic* and *Titanic*. This statement of intent was viewed with a mixture of caution and scepticism.

THE BLUE RIBAND

Right: The *Olympic* is launched from the Harland & Wolff shipyard in Belfast in 1910.

But Ismay was good to his word. The construction of two behemoths, *Olympic* and *Titanic*, began in late 1908.

The project generated huge interest from rival shipyards, most notably the Germans. Instead of trying to compete on speed, White Star decided to humiliate Cunard and Norddeutscher Lloyd with size instead. The *Olympic*-class ships would be 100 feet (30 metres) longer than the *Mauretania*, 15,000 tonnes heavier and would carry an extra 500 passengers and crew. The launch of the *Olympic* was a major international event and the yard even painted her hull light grey so it would look more impressive in the black-and-white photos of the period. Thousands of people turned out to welcome her into New York Harbour after her maiden voyage.

Titanic had been given a few modifications before her launch so she was now the largest manmade object ever to move under her own power. The ship was promptly labelled practically unsinkable to attract more passengers for her maiden voyage on the same route in April 1912. She was the last word in shipbuilding, luxury and, tragically, overconfidence.

Centre: The German ship *Kaiser Wilhelm der Grosse* threatened the dominance of Cunard and White Star.

Titanic

Titanic (and sister *Olympic*) represented the pinnacle of human achievement. At 883 feet (269 metres) in length and over 45,000 tonnes, they were bigger than anything else on the high seas by a considerable margin. The *Titanic* in particular was extremely technologically advanced for its time. Two first- and one second-class lifts allowed people to move about the ship much more easily. Her steam-powered generators gave the ship electric lighting throughout (a PA system wasn't installed but it would have been useful on the night of the tragedy). The ship also had two Marconi wireless sets to contact nearby ships and transmit messages to the shore, factors that would also play their part as the disaster unfolded.

With a list of the rich and famous onboard, *Titanic* struck an iceberg in the North Atlantic and foundered. It was an accident that never should have happened but poor luck, unusual weather conditions, excessive speed, minor design flaws, disorganisation and bad judgement all contributed to the disaster. (It is often said that large accidents never have a single cause and that they are all a chain of events, any one of which could alter the severity of the incident.)

The ship had been steaming at around 21 knots (39km/h) into an area where there was known to be ice (the ship had received several warnings from other vessels throughout that Sunday). As night closed in, the air and water

Left: The ill-fated liner at Harland & Wolff's Belfast shipyard.

But, unknown to the crew, conditions were now perfect for an unusual meteorological phenomenon known as a cold-water mirage to occur. In these special circumstances the horizon appears to rise up into the thin band of cold air and can mask objects in a ship's path. Fifty feet (15 metres) up in the crow's nest, the lookouts had been searching for ice. At around 11.00pm they noted that a slight haze had developed ahead (another sign that conditions were right for a mirage).

White Star's lookouts had all been given eye tests and they should also have been provided with binoculars but these had been misplaced in Southampton. It's doubtful binoculars would have allowed the lookouts to see the iceberg sooner but it's another piece of the jigsaw that raises a few questions (they were left behind unintentionally).

At 11.39pm, lookout Fred Fleet spotted the iceberg, grabbed the ship's bell and gave it three pulls to alert the bridge of an obstruction ahead. According to his statement to the British Inquiry, he'd seen a black object, high above the water, dead ahead. He immediately called the bridge and told Sixth Officer Moody that he had

temperatures both fell quickly as the ship entered the Labrador Current. Despite turning slightly to port to take them further south, Captain Smith did not reduce speed (it was common practice to enter ice fields at full speed because bergs could be seen at considerable distances under most atmospheric conditions, especially when waves broke against their bases).

LITTLE BOOK OF **LINERS**

seen an iceberg right ahead. This was acknowledged and Fleet noticed an almost immediate turn to port.

First Officer Murdoch ran to the open starboard bridge wing and saw the iceberg about 800 yards (730 metres) away. He immediately ordered the ship to turn hard a-starboard (as was convention at the time, the wheel rotated in the opposite direction to the way they wanted to turn) before signalling the engine room to stop, then go full astern. (On *Titanic*'s sea trial, her emergency stop had taken 850 yards or 775 metres at a slower speed so it was inevitable that she would strike the iceberg.)

Despite taking about as much avoiding action as possible, around 37 seconds after Fleet's conversation with Moody, the ship struck the iceberg. There was contact for about 10 seconds while the berg scraped along the starboard bow around 15 feet above the keel. Bad luck now played another part because the ship's hull was punctured as far back as boiler room six. If this compartment flooded, the ship would eventually sink because she could only float with her first four compartments breached, not her first five. Water flooded the ship's bow and then cascaded over the watertight

bulkheads (which didn't extend to the upper decks – a minor design flaw) into the compartments further aft like water in an ice-cube tray.

Captain Smith was roused from his cabin immediately after the collision. He then returned to the bridge so that Murdoch could brief him on what had happened. Murdoch told Smith that he'd closed the watertight doors

LITTLE BOOK OF **LINERS**

and asked designer Thomas Andrews to join them so they could inspect the damage. Andrews knew that if water was entering more than any two of the ship's watertight compartments, or if the first five compartments were breached, she was effectively doomed. Forty minutes after the collision, Andrews calculated that 16,000 tonnes of water had already entered the ship and, with water already reaching E Deck, the *Titanic* would definitely founder. Andrews gave her an hour, maybe a little more.

The ship had been built with a double hull to store water for the boilers and be used as ballast, but it was only single skin. One of the lessons of the sinking was that ships of the future should be fitted with a double-skin hull.

It has been suggested that *Titanic*'s steel was of poor quality and, following the recovery and metallurgical analysis of part of her hull, the steel used was found to be slightly brittle at low temperatures. The report concluded that a higher quality steel for her plates and stronger iron rivets with the right amount of slag might have ensured she was strong enough to survive the collision but the reality is that the shipbuilders used the best-quality materials available to them

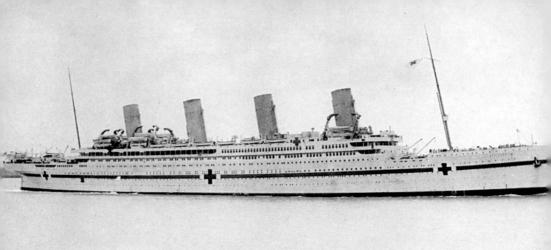

and the ship was not only strong for her time but also for ours. Indeed, many naval architects believe that the collision would probably have sunk most modern ships (the Costa Concordia disaster is a case in point and the two events bear several similarities). The ship's fate wasn't determined by her build quality but by her design.

Olympic and *Titanic* were fitted with 16 watertight compartments separated by strong bulkheads. These compartments were divided by watertight doors held in the open position by electro-magnetic latches. (The word 'watertight' is a little misleading here because the compartments were not watertight at

all. They were merely deemed to be watertight because no accident had been foreseen that could breach them.)

In the event of an emergency, the doors could be closed by a switch on the bridge. Unfortunately, whilst these transverse bulkheads offered considerable protection, they did not extend through the full height of the ship and some only reached 10 feet (three metres) above the waterline. This meant that once a number of compartments were compromised, water could seep over the top. Following the loss of the *Titanic*, the third vessel in the class, *Britannic*, had her design modified to reduce this risk, although she too foundered after striking a mine during the First World War.

More people would have been saved if the evacuation into the lifeboats had been properly organised but many left without being filled to capacity because the crew wrongly believed they couldn't be lowered fully loaded. With not enough lifeboats to cater for everyone, 1,500 people drowned (the davits could accommodate more boats but, for aesthetic reasons and because the owners believed the ship would be its own lifeboat, they weren't fitted). Only 700 were saved, of whom most were first class passengers. Those in steerage were lucky to make it to the lifeboat deck, let alone escape in one. The tragedy sent shockwaves around the world. This supposedly unsinkable ship, the pride of the British Royal Mail Fleet, had gone down in only two-and-a-half hours.

As with any story, there are villains and heroes. Captain of the Leyland Line ship *SS Californian*, Stanley Lord has been labelled the former and there is no doubt that he is one of the more controversial figures in the *Titanic* story. It has always been suggested that the *Californian* was close enough to the tragedy to see *Titanic*'s distress rockets being fired (most estimates from the evidence submitted at the two inquiries put the ships between nine and 20 miles (15 to 32 kilometres) apart. Indeed, *Titanic*'s passengers and crew spotted the lights of another ship in the distance and rockets were noted by *Californian*'s crew. Lord asked what kind of rockets they were but his crew didn't know and the ship they thought they could see appeared to be sailing away to the south.

Lord's critics argue that he should have responded immediately. Had he done so, his ship might have arrived in time to save all onboard *Titanic*. It wasn't until the following morning that Lord heard the terrible news from the *Frankfurt*, and his ship didn't arrive at the site until 8.30am. Lord was interviewed by both official inquiries, with the British concluding that he should have responded.

Although never convicted of negligence, Lord was pilloried by the media and had to spend most of the rest of his life trying to salvage his reputation. He left the Leyland Line in August the same year, although whether he resigned or was dismissed is unclear, and joined the Nitrate Producers Steamship Company in 1913. He remained with them until 1928 and died in 1962.

Carpathia, on the other hand, was lauded as the hero of the piece. Arthur Rostron's professionalism was a significant factor in the rescue of the *Titanic*'s survivors. Having heard the distress signals, Rostron quickly headed for the stricken ship but despite exceeding Carpathia's design speed they were too late to save everyone and only picked up the *Titanic*'s lifeboats. The *Carpathia* then delivered 700 survivors to New York. Rostron gave evidence at both the US and British inquiries and was presented with a silver cup by grateful survivors. He continued his career with Cunard, becoming a Commander of the Order of the British Empire in 1919 and receiving his knighthood seven years later. He became Commodore of the Cunard Line before retiring in 1931. He died in 1940.

Titanic's designer, Thomas Andrews, and captain, Edward Smith, went down with the ship but Bruce Ismay climbed into a lifeboat and was rescued by the *Carpathia* the following morning. It was seen as an act of extreme cowardice and he was also pilloried mercilessly in the press. The official enquiry then exonerated Harland & Wolff but hammered the board of trade's outdated regulations governing the number of

In 1992, the British Marine Accident Investigation Branch reviewed all the available evidence and concluded that the *Californian* did not see the *Titanic* itself because the distance between them was too great but her crew did see *Titanic*'s rockets so should have acted.

The captain of the Cunard liner

lifeboats and the passage of such mighty ships through ice.

As so often happens after a major disaster, new laws and rules were immediately drawn up. Liners of the future would have to carry lifeboats with enough capacity for everyone onboard, irrespective of the class in which they were travelling. But the damage to the British psyche had already been done. The people had put their trust in money and power and the mechanisation of the age, but in one moment their hopes of a better future had been dashed. Some even believed it was the turning point that heralded the end of the empire.

The arrival of the car and aeroplane diverted some attention away from the tragedy but naval power was never far from the agenda. Kaiser Wilhelm's Germany was still building for war. In the industrial heartland of the Ruhr and Essen, workers churned out tanks and guns and the steel plates for her battleships.

TITANIC

Centre: The *Carpathia* unloads Titanic survivors in New York.

50

The Liners at War

The director of the Hamburg-America Line, Albert Ballin, pleaded with the Kaiser not to commandeer his ships if war erupted. He even went as far as to try brokering a deal whereby Britain and Germany competed to build greater liners but resisted the temptation to best each other's naval fleets. His appeal initially appeared to have worked. Hamburg-America launched the *Imperator* shortly afterwards. She was the longest ship ever built, and the first to exceed 50,000 tonnes. Together with her sisters *SS Vaterland* and *SS Bismarck* (which, at 956 feet or 290 metres, took over as the longest ship), Ballin hoped the trio would trump the competition.

Ballin wasn't just a visionary shipbuilder. He made sure immigrants arriving in Hamburg seeking a life in the New World had somewhere to live for up to two weeks before sailing. He provided medical centres and food along with the accommodation. But Hamburg-America soon found itself competing with another German company, Norddeutscher Lloyd. There was no time for the rivalry to pique the public's interest, however. Archduke Franz Ferdinand was assassinated in Sarajevo in the summer of 1914 and the world was plunged into war. The Blue Riband wouldn't change hands again until long after hostilities had ceased.

As soon as war was declared, all German ships were placed on a war footing. Most of them had already rehearsed the drills required to transform them into auxiliary cruisers, and their captains had been briefed for at least a decade prior to the outbreak of hostilities.

The plan didn't get off to a good start, however, because only five passenger ships made it back to Germany while the remaining forty or so were impounded in neutral ports. With the *Vaterland* stuck in New York, the *Wilhelm der Grosse* sank several allied ships before heading for Northwest Africa to take on more coal. She was spotted by the British

Right: The German High Command warns passengers travelling from the US to Europe that British ships might be attacked.

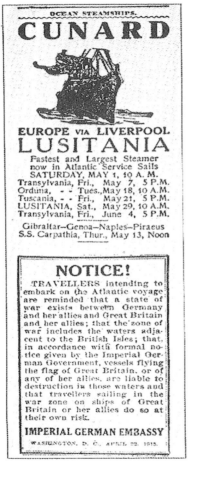

OCEAN STEAMSHIPS.

CUNARD

EUROPE VIA LIVERPOOL.
LUSITANIA

Fastest and Largest Steamer
now in Atlantic Service Sails
SATURDAY, MAY 1, 10 A. M.
Transylvania, Fri., May 7, 5 P.M.
Orduna, - - Tues., May 18, 10 A.M.
Tuscania, - - Fri., May 21, 5 P.M.
LUSITANIA, Sat., May 29, 10 A.M.
Transylvania, Fri., June 4, 5 P.M.

Gibraltar—Genoa—Naples—Piraeus
S.S. Carpathia, Thur., May 13, Noon

NOTICE!

TRAVELLERS intending to embark on the Atlantic voyage are reminded that a state of war exists between Germany and her allies and Great Britain and her allies; that the zone of war includes the waters adjacent to the British Isles; that, in accordance with formal notice given by the Imperial German Government, vessels flying the flag of Great Britain, or of any of her allies, are liable to destruction in those waters and that travellers sailing in the war zone on ships of Great Britain or her allies do so at their own risk.

IMPERIAL GERMAN EMBASSY

WASHINGTON, D. C., APRIL 22, 1915.

cruiser *HMS Highflyer* and engaged, with the liner losing the battle and sinking. It was a sad end for the ship that had taken the Blue Riband and had ushered in a growing, albeit peaceful, rivalry between Britain and Germany at the turn of the century.

First Lord of the Admiralty Winston Churchill immediately ordered the Royal Navy to blockade Germany and prevent their fleet from leaving their home ports. He hoped this would eventually starve the enemy into submission. The Germans countered by ordering their U-boat fleet to attack British ships. Their captains initially complied with tradition and warned ships before firing upon them. This gave the crew the chance to escape in the lifeboats. But all that was about to change – total war was on the horizon.

Mauretania and one of her sisters, *Aquitania*, were quickly transformed into armed auxiliary cruisers. Their lavish interiors were stripped and they were equipped with heavy guns. Although she was initially recruited for the same role, the *Lusitania* was then spared because the line still needed a ship to manage the trans-Atlantic run and using the liners for war was a huge drain on resources, particularly coal. So she was repainted in her familiar colours and dispatched to familiar territory. (*Mauretania* and *Aquitania* were only used as troop transports thereafter, a tradition that had begun during the Crimean War and which continued during the Boer War as Britain recruited soldiers from all corners of the empire and ferried them to the war zones on the liners of the day. It was not uncommon for these ships to be troop transports on the way out and hospital ships on the way home.)

The German High Command feared that Britain could be re-supplied with weapons and troops from abroad so it adopted a policy of unrestricted war on the high seas. They even used advertising space in American newspapers to warn potential passengers that it was not safe to cross the Atlantic on the liners because they would be attacked. The British could have ordered their fleets not to enter the dangerous waters around the Channel to the south of Ireland but they chose not to. The stage was set for one of the most controversial episodes in maritime history.

The sinking of the *Lusitania*

In May 1915, the *Lusitania* was nearing the end of another Atlantic crossing when she received a warning that there were U-boats off southern Ireland. Despite having great confidence in his ship, and knowing it could outrun any U-boat, Captain William Turner took the prudent decision to head for the safety of Queenstown until the threat had passed. But his ship had already been spotted (and identified) by Kapitan-Leutnant Walther Schwieger in *U-20*. Since February, Germany had stated that they were at total war and ships in the exclusion zone around the British Isles would not be warned before being fired upon.

U-20 shadowed the liner but was in danger of losing touch when one of the *Lusitania*'s evasive zigzags took her straight into the submarine's path. *U-20* fired a single torpedo that struck the ship just forward of the bridge on her starboard side. The impact was serious but probably wouldn't

Above: The *Lusitania* enters New York Harbour on her maiden voyage in 1907.

have sunk her. However, a second much larger explosion then rocked the *Lusitania* and she sank within 20 minutes, taking 1,198 people down with her.

The cause of the secondary explosion has long been debated. Schwieger maintained until his dying day that he only fired one torpedo (and his log appears to verify his account), so it seems that the explosion must have come from within the ship. There

are three possibilities: one of the ship's boilers exploded, which was extremely unlikely; there was a sympathetic coal-dust eruption, which is possible; or that the ship was carrying munitions to help the war effort, which is quite probable. In 1993, Doctor Robert Ballard, discoverer of the *Titanic*'s wreck, dived to the *Lusitania* and concluded that the torpedo had hit an empty fuel bunker. The impact would have disturbed highly explosive coal

dust, which could then have ignited and blown the ship apart, although many still believe she was carrying munitions and millions of small-calibre rounds have since been recovered.

Whatever the cause, the engagement backfired spectacularly on the German High Command because the deaths of American citizens, many of them children, eventually drew the United States into the conflict. Although Woodrow Wilson didn't immediately declare war, he sent the Kaiser a strong message of intent and warned that if any more ships were targeted, they would reap the consequences. Germany took no notice and continued its aggressive policy of sinking passenger ships. The US initially retaliated by impounding German liners. They then converted them into troop transports and declared war. Two million men joined the war effort and they eventually pummelled Germany into submission.

LITTLE BOOK OF **LINERS**

Another casualty of war: the *Britannic*

Left: The SS *Ile de France* in about 1935.

*T*itanic's younger sister was probably going to have been christened *Gigantic* but the disaster had been felt so keenly that such a grand name was deemed unnecessary. She was renamed *Britannic* and was immediately converted into a hospital ship to tend to the troops fighting in the Dardanelles in the Eastern Mediterranean. In the first few months of the Gallipoli Campaign more than 100,000 soldiers were treated on these hospital ships.

With the campaign an unmitigated disaster, the *Britannic* was steaming towards the theatre of war in November 1916 when she struck a mine just south of the island of Kea in the Aegean Sea. Although her hull and watertight compartments had been modified in the wake of the *Titanic* disaster, the ship was mortally wounded and sank in just under an hour. Some of her watertight doors

failed to close and most of her portholes were open to air the wards, so she took on water quickly and promptly foundered. Thankfully, of the 1,066 people onboard, more than 1,000 were saved.

The *Britannic* may have been the largest ship sunk during the war, but she was by no means the only White Star casualty. Indeed, the war was particularly brutal for the line's great ships: the *Arabic* was torpedoed and sunk off the Old Head of Kinsale (not far from where the *Lusitania* met her end) in August 1915; the *Cymric* was sunk in the same area by the infamous *U-20* in early 1916; the *Laurentic* struck mines off the coast of Northern Ireland and sank with the loss of over 350 lives; and the *Afric* and the *Delphic* were both sunk in the English Channel in 1917. Many more ships were so badly damaged that they were retired.

Cunard were not spared the horrors of war either: the *Ultonia*, *Ivernia*, *Franconia*, *Laconia*, *Andania* and *Aurania* were all sunk by enemy submarines and the *Alaunia* foundered after striking a mine in 1916.

Albert Ballin committed suicide two days before the end of the First World War rather than see his magnificent ships ceded to the British as part of the armistice. Those ships were immediately put to work ferrying troops home. The *Vaterland*, now rechristened the *Leviathan*, once took 14,000 men back to the United States, then the largest number of people ever to sail on a single vessel.

In 1919 the powers met in Versailles, Paris, to decide Germany's fate. Having lost a number of liners during the war, the White Star Line was given *Bismarck*, which they renamed *Majestic*. The *Imperator* was ceded to Cunard and rechristened *Berengaria*. Countless refugees seeking new lives in Canada, the United States and Australia (up to 30,000 people sailed each week from Europe to the New World) meant that these ships were in constant demand after the war. The first port of call for many of these immigrants was Ellis Island. Here they would be checked for illness, disease, mental instability and lice, before they would be allowed to enter the United States. More than 100 million people can now trace their ancestry

Far Left: A damaged *U-20* aground in Denmark in 1916.

to these immigrants arriving at the end of the war. There was trouble on the horizon for the American liners, however. The numbers of immigrants were proving a drain on the economy so their numbers were restricted, and prohibition meant that they could not serve alcohol. The foreign lines started to clean up so the Americans countered by registering their ships abroad and then organising boozy tourist trips to exotic locations.

With the immigration trade a thing of the past, the super-liners dropped their steerage class and renamed it tourist class. Travel back across the Atlantic was now affordable and exciting and many middle-class Americans made the trip to see the historic European sites and to experience the nightlife of Paris and Rome.

But these great liners had been built before the war and they were expensive to run and maintain. White Star and Cunard retired many of their aging fleet and introduced smaller, faster ships for the North Atlantic run. The Germans followed suit and Hamburg-America was soon one of the more profitable companies operating on the route. The French took a different stance and launched the mighty *Île de France*, at 44,000 tonnes and nearly 800 feet (240 metres) the largest ship built since the war. The ship was so beautifully decorated that it raised the bar for both Cunard and White Star.

Norddeutscher Lloyd also had their ships confiscated at the end of the war but the US government then compensated them and they used the money to build two new greyhounds, the *SS Bremen* and the *SS Europa*. By the end of the 1920s, the world economy was in a fragile state and passenger numbers declined, but the Germans were determined to counter the global downturn by going bigger and better. The *Bremen* and *Europa* were now the greatest ships in the world, and they regained the Blue Riband for Germany, the latter maintaining an average speed during the North Atlantic crossing just shy of 28 knots (52km/h). But Cunard was not to be outdone. The company approached John Brown for two new liners to challenge the Germans. The golden age of the liners had begun.

Centre:
Hamburg-
America's mighty
Imperator.

The Great Duel

The British responded to the threat from the *Bremen* and *Europa* by starting work on two magnificent new Cunarders in late 1930. At 80,000 tonnes they would be the largest and fastest ships afloat. The French also decided to get in on the act and reprise the *Île de France* in the shape of the longest liner then built: the *Normandie*. The French and British thus became locked in a battle to take on the Germans.

The economic downturn forced Cunard to have a rethink, however, and they laid off more than 3,000 men. The massive hulls were nearly complete but they were then simply left to rust. Britain was out of the race. The Italians, who had only ever been bit-part players, also

appeared to be out but Mussolini merged the country's three shipbuilders and they produced the magnificent greyhound *Rex* that immediately took the Blue Riband. Together with her stylish and luxurious running mate, *Conte di Savoia*, the ships brought Italy to the forefront of the desirable Atlantic run.

In 1932 the French finally launched the 83,000-tonne, 1,029-foot (314-metre) *Normandie*. Her beautiful raked bow and streamlined superstructure left the competition looking slow and outdated. Her lavish interior included elegant public rooms, a theatre, winter garden, a first-class dining room that rivalled the Hall of Mirrors in the Palace of Versailles and could seat 700 people, and a café/grill that

Above: The enormous *SS Normandie* is put through her paces in 1932.

could be converted into a nightclub.

In 1934, the British government oversaw the merger of White Star and Cunard; the British were back in the race after a two-year hiatus and they promptly set about renovating the rusting hulks. This signalled the end of the Great Depression and the magnificent *Queen Mary* was the result. Her arrival sparked a great duel between the two largest ships in history.

The new Queen was a giant herself and displaced nearly 82,000 tonnes when fitted out. She was 10 feet (three metres)

Above: The enormous *SS Normandie* is put through her paces in 1932.

LITTLE BOOK OF **LINERS**

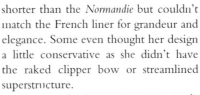

shorter than the *Normandie* but couldn't match the French liner for grandeur and elegance. Some even thought her design a little conservative as she didn't have the raked clipper bow or streamlined superstructure.

Six months later, 200,000 people turned out to watch the wife of George V christen her namesake before the ship was launched into the River Clyde. It would take another two years before she was ready to sail on her maiden voyage, however, by which time the *Normandie* would already be plying the North Atlantic with 3,000 fare-paying passengers of all classes. The French downplayed rumours that she was going for the Blue Riband on her maiden voyage but she averaged 30 knots (56km/h) and made the crossing in a shade over four days to claim the record. It was another dent to British morale. They needed to counter the threat with a record-breaking run from the *Queen Mary*.

No other ship in history was under such close scrutiny on her maiden voyage. She lost valuable time when she was forced to slow in thick fog but she then answered her critics by reaching 33 knots (61km/h). Sadly, she missed the

Left: The *Queen Mary* brings American troops back to New York Harbour at the end of WWII in June 1945.

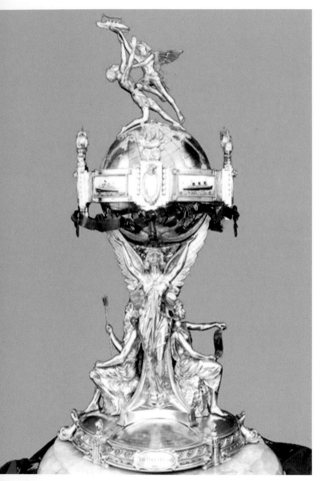

record by a matter of minutes but that didn't dampen the enthusiasm at home and abroad for such a magnificent ship. Indeed, it was only a matter of time before she reclaimed the Blue Riband for Britain. In so doing, she became the first ship to make the crossing in fewer than four days. The elation was short-lived because *Normandie* regained the title with a 31.2-knot (58km/h) crossing shortly afterwards. *Queen Mary* had the last laugh, however, with a 31.6-knot (59km/h) average speed in 1937, a record that stood for 15 years.

The Hales Trophy

In 1935 Harold Hales commissioned a Sheffield goldsmith to produce a solid silver four-foot (1.2m), 100-pound (40kg) trophy that would be awarded to the fastest ship crossing the Atlantic, and therefore the holder of the Blue Riband. The magnificent piece of silverware was decorated with galleons, ocean liners and the gods of the sea.

Hales stipulated that he wanted the Blue Riband rules changed. Previously,

the title was awarded to the ship with the fastest average speed on the westbound leg from Europe to America, but he insisted the trophy should go to any surface passenger ship with the fastest speed in either direction. The trophy was first presented to the Italian liner *Rex*, and then to the *Normandie*. The *Queen Mary*'s captain refused to accept it after his ship's record-breaking run because he didn't believe the ship was racing to win a prize. Hales saw this as an affront to his generosity and changed the rules again so that the trophy could not be won by a British vessel.

The *SS United States* upped the record average speed to 34.5 knots (64km/h) in 1952 and the trophy was displayed at the line's offices until the ship's retirement in 1969. The next assault on the record came from Richard Branson's *Challenger*

II powerboat in 1986 but, although he made the eastbound crossing at record speed, he was not awarded the trophy because it was not a commercial passenger vessel. Branson was then trumped by the Italian powerboat *Destriero*, which clocked 53 knots (98km/h).

In 1990, the crew of the 242-foot (74-metre) catamaran *Hoverspeed Great Britain* confirmed with the trustees of the Hales Trophy that their vessel was eligible (British-built passenger ships were back in their good books) and went for the record. They succeeded with an average speed of 37 knots (68km/h). The current holder of the trophy is *Cat-Link V*, which averaged 41 knots (76km/h) in 1998, although the *SS United States* is still, as a commercial passenger liner, considered the holder of the prestigious Blue Riband.

Round Two of the Duel

The 1930s were a period when attracting the wealthy and famous could do your image the world of good. Cunard White Star repeatedly published passenger lists so everyone would know who was travelling with them. The press would then turn up as the ship made port to photograph the VIPs disembarking, all in the name of good publicity.

The *Queen Mary* also won the battle for profits. As lavish as the *Normandie* was, many felt the décor was overdone and they preferred the understated British-ness of the rival Queen with its unrivalled service. But this was an era in which Nazi Germany would also compete for the money and prestige on offer. Hitler insisted that the country's infrastructure and trade be brought up to date, and their motorways, navy and fleet of aircraft were soon the envy of the world. The German labour front boosted their industry and economy, and members of the Nazi Party were soon being offered cheap cruises on several fine ships in Hitler's 'strength through joy' scheme.

The initiative worked and passenger numbers soared. The added bonus was that the workers spread the national socialist word further across Europe, particularly to Italy, which embraced many of their ideals. Such was the popularity of the cruises that the government ordered two new liners. The *Wilhelm Gustloff* was designed from the keel up as a cruise ship, and was the first one-class vessel to offer the same standard of service and accommodation for her crew. Two years later a second ship, the *Robert Ley*, entered service. Hitler himself joined the ship for her maiden voyage, the publicity surrounding the sailing immediately being used for propaganda at home.

In 1938, Britain garnered some much-needed publicity for her own shipbuilding industry by launching *Queen Mary*'s sister, the *Queen Elizabeth*, in front of 300,000 people at the John Brown shipyard in Scotland. She was another ship conceived and built during peacetime but Europe was again on the brink of war and she would not see civilian service for seven years.

Hitler's blitzkrieg had immediate consequences for the liners crossing the North Atlantic. On the day Britain

declared war on Germany, U-30 torpedoed the passenger liner *Athenia* off Ireland (the first Allied casualty of the war). Although only around 100 people were killed, the intent was clear. And, to add insult to injury, the *SS Bremen* ignored her distress calls. The ship eventually sank the following morning. The legality of the sinking was immediately questioned because the ship was an unarmed passenger liner.

Unlike the *Lusitania* 24 years previously, the *Athenia* was not converted into a troop transport and was not carrying munitions. Admiral Dönitz had insisted that all ships be identified before they were fired upon, and under no circumstances were civilian vessels to be attacked. Oberleutnant Fritz-Julius Lemp claimed that because the ship was running with few lights on a zigzag course far from the traditional routes she must be a troop transport or armed merchant cruiser so he

attacked without being certain. For this reason, the Third Reich covered up the attack and claimed instead that Britain had sunk the ship to bring Canada and the United States into the war.

Churchill may have been secretly pleased that the *Lusitania* sinking had just that effect in the First World War, but to torpedo and sink one of your own ships with heavy loss of life was unthinkable. The sinking was an unmitigated propaganda disaster for Germany because it proved how low she would stoop to gain outright victory. Fearing reprisals, when the German ship *SS Columbus* was sighted by the British in December 1939, the crew set her on fire and scuttled her to prevent her falling into enemy hands.

The world was once again at war, and in times of total war the normal rules of engagement were often forgotten. The days of the great ocean liners seemed to be numbered.

Right: The *Rex* is overflown by a pair of American B-17 bombers.

A Return to War

Hitler's U-boats were soon blockading Britain and the government feared that they would target the as yet unfinished *Queen Elizabeth* that was still in Scotland. Word was deliberately spread that the liner was being transferred to dry dock in Southampton but this was merely a ruse in case enemy spies got wind of her true destination, which was New York. The deception worked. Nazi bombers patrolled the Solent for the next few days but by then the ship had made her escape. Indeed her sea trials involved racing across the Atlantic avoiding U-boats.

When she reached America she was tied up alongside her sister, *Queen Mary*, and great rival, *Normandie*. In April 1940, the *Queen Mary* sailed for Australia and

was pressed into service as a troop ship. She was joined by the *Mauretania* and *Aquitania* in what became a fleet of troop transports. The liners were soon packed with thousands of Australian and Kiwi troops on their way to fight in another World War.

This was a delicate mission balancing the risk of being sunk by a U-boat or enemy ship against the reward of recruiting thousands of troops to help with the war effort. Conditions aboard the convoy were not pleasant. The ships had been stripped of all their finery and, having been built to ply the cold North Atlantic, did not have air conditioning. Sailing in muggy equatorial conditions forced many men to sleep in the open air

to escape the foul bowels of the ships.

By the time they arrived back in Britain, they received news that France had capitulated. Hitler's next target was Britain. London was soon reduced to a burning ruin in the Blitz but the country refused to buckle. Churchill dispatched another fleet of liners to the Middle East to counter the Italian thrust, but this only depleted the number of fighting men at home. More needed to be drafted in from the colonies so the *Queen Elizabeth* left New York and headed down under. When she returned, the United States would also be at war.

After the attack on Pearl Harbour in December 1941, President Roosevelt immediately seized the *Normandie* and converted her into a troop transport. But a fire broke out during the conversion and the great ship eventually capsized due to all the water pumped into her in an attempt to stop the fire spreading. It was an ignominious end for such a magnificent ship. The ship might never have capsized at all had port director Adolphus Andrews listened to the ship's designer, Vladimir Yourkevitch. He instructed the fire crews to open the fire doors to allow water to escape (as well as opening the sea cocks). This would allow the ship to settle into the harbour upright, which would make pumping the water out much easier. His suggestions were ignored and the ship's fate was sealed.

The *Queen Mary* was now on her way

from Boston to the Asia-Pacific theatre with 8,000 troops. German radio reported that she'd been sunk by a U-boat with the loss of 15,000 men but this was yet another PR disaster for the Reich. Over the next two years a million American troops would arrive in Sydney to help protect the British colony from the Japanese. This influx had a tremendous impact on the culture of a country that was still a little behind the rest of the world in fashion, sophistication and attitude.

In October 1942 the *Queen Mary* accidentally sank one of her escorts, the light cruiser *HMS Curacoa*. With U-boats patrolling the seas, the *Queen Mary* was instructed not to stop after the collision because she was carrying thousands of American troops. More than 200 people died before they could be rescued by the remaining ships in the convoy.

In November the same year, the largest flotilla yet assembled (170 warships and 350 merchant vessels) transported men and machinery from Britain and the United States as part of Operation Torch, the Allied attempt to wrest control of French North Africa from the Germans and Italians under Rommel. The convoy landed a little late but the influx pushed the Axis Powers east and boosted morale among the Allies.

The Atlantic convoys may have eventually brought enough American men to Europe to launch the D-Day invasion but the ships were often slow-moving and made easy targets for the marauding U-boats. The two mighty Queens seemed to be indestructible, however. For most of the war they sailed without naval escorts and delivered more than a million men to the war effort. Slicing through the waves at more than 30 knots (56km/h), they were simply too quick for the U-boats and neither was ever attacked. Churchill couldn't praise the ships highly enough and even claimed they'd shortened the conflict by a year.

These crossings were not without incident, however. In December 1942 the *Queen Mary* was carrying more than 16,000 troops (a record that still stands for the most people ever on a ship) when she was struck by a rogue wave during a gale off the coast of Scotland. From eyewitness accounts and the damage she sustained, it's estimated that the 92-foot (28-metre) wave heeled her over to 52 degrees, only three degrees short of the point at which she would have capsized. On hearing about the near catastrophe, American novelist Paul Gallico penned the novel

Far Left: Fire rages throughout the *Normandie*. She would soon capsize.

A RETURN TO WAR

Far Right: More than 9,400 people died when the *Wilhelm Gustloff* sank after being torpedoed by a Russian submarine in January 1945.

The Poseidon Adventure, which chronicled the struggle of a few survivors after their passenger liner was capsized by a wave generated by an undersea earthquake. The 1972 film of the same name saw the *Queen Mary* double as the *SS Poseidon*.

The Queens may have been lucky but a number of the great liners did pay the ultimate price during the war. The *SS Rex*, for example, was commandeered by the Germans in 1944. They planned to use it to block the harbour entrance to Trieste but a squadron of Royal Air Force Beaufighters attacked and sank her with rocket salvos in September.

The German flagship *Wilhelm Gustloff* was another ship that didn't survive hostilities. She was torpedoed by a Russian submarine, *S-13*, in the Baltic in January 1945. The ship was crammed with refugees and wounded soldiers and the sinking was the worst maritime disaster in history. An estimated 9,400 people perished, most in the icy water when she sank, but a good proportion were crushed as they tried to escape the bowels of the ship.

Another German ship, the *SS Cap Arcona*, had been the pride of the Hamburg-South American line. She was taken over by the German navy to help evacuate troops from Prussia and prisoners from the concentration camps when she was sunk by the RAF in the Baltic. It was a tragic episode because many concentration camp survivors lost their lives. Faulty intelligence led the pilots to believe that SS officers were escaping on the ship instead. They even strafed the survivors in the water believing them to be the last remnants of the Nazi Party. In all, around 5,000 people were killed.

The war ended a couple of days later and Cunard immediately set about renewing interest in the North Atlantic run with a maiden peacetime voyage for the *Queen Elizabeth*. The *Queen Mary* then joined her on the twice-weekly service from Southampton to New York. They were soon taking the lion's share of the profits and the older liners like *Aquitania* were retired because they were no longer profitable.

There were now two reasons for the Americans to enter the fray. They wanted their share of the route and they also felt they needed a large troop transport in case another war was on the horizon. The result was the last great greyhound of the seas, the mighty *SS United States*, which single-handedly dragged luxury travel into the modern era.

LITTLE BOOK OF **LINERS**

The End of an Era

The American government made three demands of the *SS United States*: she must be fast, safe and able to convert to a troop transport in record time. On the first issue, she was in a different class to everything that had gone before. Designer William Francis Gibbs fitted the ship with 248,000-horsepower steam turbines scheduled for use in the navy's latest aircraft carriers so she was much more powerful than her contemporaries. In July 1952 she averaged 35.5 knots (66km/h) and shaved an incredible 10 hours off the *Queen Mary*'s North Atlantic crossing, capturing the Blue Riband for America. For the first time in a century, the US was a serious competitor on the world's most popular shipping route.

She was also safe. To avoid the risk of fire, no wood was used for her frame, accessories, décor or interior. Instead, her fixtures and fittings were made almost entirely from glass, metal and fibreglass so, despite being 990 feet (300 metres) long, at only 47,000 tonnes she was considerably lighter than her competitors (her superstructure was mainly constructed from aluminium, which also helped save weight). And she could be converted into a troop ship in as little as two days.

This was the 1950s and competition for the North Atlantic run was about to peak, with the *SS United States* and

Above: Cunard's flagship *Queen Elizabeth 2*.

the two Queens battling for supremacy. But there was a new threat to the profitability of the route, and it came from the air.

Travel by jet aircraft may have been in its infancy but a trans-Atlantic crossing in the new Boeing 707s could be made in as little as eight hours. On a ship, half the fun was the journey itself, but for business people needing to cross as quickly as possible, air travel was the way forward. By the end of the decade more people would be making the trip by air than by sea, and on some of the ships the crew outnumbered the passengers. It was the beginning of the end for the great liners.

By 1965, the impact of relatively cheap air travel was beginning to bite and Cunard was operating at a significant loss. This was a big blow as the new *Queen Elizabeth 2* was only a couple of years from entering service. The *Queen Mary* was the first to feel the squeeze and she was retired to Long Beach, California, in 1967 when the port's bid

Above: The *SS France* moored in Hong Kong in 1974.

of US$3.5 million (then £1.2 million) was accepted over the amount offered by a Japanese scrap merchant. It was a quiet end for a ship that had made 1,000 Atlantic crossings with more than two million passengers. The ship is now a mix of hotel, museum and tourist attraction.

Queen Elizabeth was next to be retired. She was sold to a group of Philadelphia-based businessmen in 1968. She was sold again two years later to the Orient Overseas Line in Hong Kong. C.Y. Tung then set about converting the ship into a floating university in Victoria Harbour, but disaster struck in 1972 when a fire gutted the interior and the water used to extinguish the blaze caused the ship

construction of a freight terminal at the end of the last century. It was a sad end for one of the world's last great liners. (The ship was the largest wreck until the *Costa Concordia* hit rocks and settled onto her side off the Italian island of Isola del Giglio in January 2012.)

Perhaps hoping to rekindle some of the lost interest in the great liners of the 1930s, Cunard launched the *Queen Elizabeth 2* in 1969. Her introduction to service saw her threaten the French Line ship *SS France*. Another duel seemed to be on the cards.

France

Two 35,000-tonne French ships were originally ordered to challenge the *SS United States* and to take on Cunard's new Queen, but President Charles de Gaulle stepped in and insisted that one enormous liner be built to boost French nationalism, which was taking a hit due to the ongoing War of Algerian Independence. With the *Île de France* and *SS Liberté* being retired, the *Normandie* was clearly the benchmark.

The ship would enter service in difficult times so she had to be fast and

to capsize, much like the *Normandie*. There is some speculation that the fire was started deliberately as several seemed to break out simultaneously, and Tung had insured the ship for three times its current value…

The wreck was deemed a hazard to navigation and was gradually broken up. Her remains were finally buried during

economical to counter the hike in oil prices and the threat from air travel. The *SS France*'s keel was laid down in Saint-Nazaire in 1957 but most of her hull and superstructure were prefabricated in cities around the country before being assembled in the shipyard. She had a double bottom, extended fuel tanks and twin stabilisers. She was launched three years later by Yvonne de Gaulle and completed her sea trials at an impressive 35 knots (65km/h) in 1961, prompting

LITTLE BOOK OF **LINERS**

first Atlantic crossing in 1962 and was soon ferrying the rich and famous to and from the United States. The 1970s brought the *France* mixed fortunes, however. The Atlantic run was no longer profitable as passengers took to the skies and the oil crisis meant she was expensive to maintain, but the line countered by sending the ship on winter cruises to the tropics during the low season on the North Atlantic.

There were problems with the ship's design for cruising in warmer climates, however. Deck space was limited, neither of the two swimming pools was open-air, and she was too large to navigate the Panama Canal. Despite these issues, cruises on the *France* were increasingly popular and she embarked on her first world tour in 1972. She was paving the way for the next generation of giant ships.

Queen Elizabeth 2

husband Charles to claim she could win back the Blue Riband.

At 1,035 feet (316 metres) long, she was a true giant, although her unique design saved weight and she was only 70,000 tonnes. She made her

Queen Elizabeth 2 joined the fray in 1969. Cunard knew it had to retire its aging Queens but didn't want to cede the Atlantic run to the *France* so it gambled on building a single

£80-million liner to replace them. The company decided that *QE2* should be smaller, more efficient and cheaper to operate than her predecessors, but they also insisted that she run at the same speed, be able to enter more ports and be maintained by a smaller crew.

Meeting these demands was extremely difficult but the new flagship was a triumph of design and engineering. She was 963 feet (294 metres) long, weighed 70,000 tonnes, could reach 34 knots (63km/h), and catered for 1,900 passengers in a virtually classless environment. She was launched by Queen Elizabeth II from the John Brown shipyard in Scotland in 1967, fitted out the following year and embarked on her maiden voyage in 1969.

Her 110,000 horsepower steam turbines were plagued with problems however so, despite them being technically advanced and powering her across 2.6 million miles (4.2 million km) of ocean, they were eventually replaced with nine 120-tonne German diesel engines producing 130,000 horsepower. Her fixed-pitch propellers were also replaced with variable-pitch screws. With this new configuration, the ship saw a 35 percent fuel saving and could run at top speed on only seven of her nine diesels. Remaining power could then be diverted to run the desalination plant and provide extra heat throughout the ship.

In 1982 the *QE2* carried 3,000 troops of the Fifth Infantry to the South Atlantic to help retake the Falkland Islands. This required a major conversion in Southampton that saw the public lounges become dormitories, all the carpets covered with hardboard and three helicopter pads installed. She returned triumphantly the following month and was met on Southampton Water by Queen Elizabeth, the Queen Mother, onboard the Royal Yacht *Britannia*.

The ship then underwent a minor refit as she was converted back to civilian duty. This included having her hull painted a light grey but this proved unpopular with passengers and she reverted to the traditional black shortly afterwards.

Canberra

The *QE2* wasn't the only ship used to ferry troops during the war. The P&O cruise ship *Canberra* also transported fighting men to the islands.

With her innovative turbo-electric propulsion system, the 818-foot (250-metre), 45,000-tonne *Canberra* had been designed and built as a liner in the early 1960s but the decline in passenger numbers and the ease with which Australia and New Zealand could now be reached by aircraft immediately saw her run become unsustainable. To capitalise on the increasing tourist market, *Canberra* was brought in for a refit in 1974, although the amount of work needed to convert her into a dedicated cruise ship was minimal.

She was cruising the Mediterranean when the Falklands War broke out, so she was immediately recalled to Southampton for a minor refit so that she could also accommodate troops. She then transported the Parachute Regiment and the Royal Marines into the danger zone (*QE2* was deemed too valuable and vulnerable to approach the islands). She anchored in San Carlos Water as part of the landings that would retake the islands and soon became a target for the Argentine air force.

Thankfully, the liner was not badly damaged because the pilots tended to concentrate on the naval vessels rather than the troop transports, but it was still a narrow escape. The *Canberra* then took on *QE2*'s troops at South Georgia and ferried them back to the Falklands to end the Argentine resistance. She returned home to a heroine's welcome in July and immediately had to be refitted to keep pace with the new breed of cruise ships.

Because of her role in the war she was extremely popular with tourists, and passenger numbers remained high until the early 1990s. By then she was showing her age, however. High fuel consumption and general running costs saw her withdrawn from service and scrapped in Pakistan in 1997.

When the *QE2* returned from the Falklands she also went in for a refit. Her problem engines were swapped for the new diesels and her passenger accommodation was upgraded. These improvements were expected to last another 20 years until she was retired but there were problems immediately. Her boilers malfunctioned and then an electrical fire caused the cancellation of a cruise in 1984. Because she was the flagship of the line and a symbol of national prestige, she was repaired and re-entered service. She ran aground in

1992 on uncharted rocks near Martha's Vineyard and had to make more repairs. Two years later, Cunard decided to send her to Hamburg for another refit to counter the rise of the dedicated cruise ships.

The *QE2* then had all her public rooms refurbished and was given a royal blue hull. Despite being immediately struck by a 90-foot (27-metre) rogue wave, she marked her return to service with a number of records: by her 30th anniversary cruise in 1999 she'd clocked up nearly 1,200 voyages, over five million sailing miles (the equivalent of circumnavigating the globe 223 times), and her two millionth passenger.

Cunard was then taken over by the Carnival Corporation, with the company bringing the *QE2* in for a $30 million refit in late 1999. As well as having her promenades adapted for the cruise market, her public areas were once again upgraded and her colour scheme was returned to Cunard's original black hull and white superstructure.

Her days were numbered, however. In 2004 the new flagship *Queen Mary 2* took over the trans-Atlantic run and confined her older sister to cruising the Mediterranean with a single annual world tour. Later that same year she became Cunard's longest serving express liner (trumping the 35 years *Aquitania* spent in service), while the following year she became the longest serving Cunarder of all time (passing the *Scythia*'s record).

In 2007 she created another moment of history when she met up with *Queen Mary 2* in Sydney Harbour, the first time the two running mates had been berthed alongside one another, and the first time Cunard's two Queens had met in Sydney since the original *Queen Elizabeth* and *Queen Mary* had been dispatched to collect Australian troops in 1941. When she was returning home, it was announced that the *QE2* had been sold to a Dubai-based investment company Ististhmar for $100 million (£70 million).

A farewell tour was hastily arranged so that the ship could meet the latest Cunarder, *Queen Victoria* in New York, which coincided with the arrival of *Queen Mary 2*. When the three joined up again in Southampton in early 2008, it was the last time they would be together. *QE2* was then escorted around the British Isles before she

headed back to Southampton for the last time. On entering the Solent she ran aground on the Brambles Sandbank but was re-floated an hour later. The Duke of Edinburgh then inspected her before she was decommissioned.

For the last four years the great ship has been moored in Port Rashid, Dubai. Despite plans to convert her into a hotel or museum, or even to put her back into service, the global economic downturn has left her with an uncertain future.

The *France*, on the other hand, was almost put out of commission during the oil crisis. The government realised that a quadrupling of prices would put the line out of business so they poured money into the Concorde project instead. The crew objected and took the unusual action of striking while onboard. They refused to let the ship dock in Le Havre and 1,200 passengers had to be taken off by tender instead. With the ship blocking the harbour entrance, the crew knew they held the advantage and demanded a 35 percent wage increase. The standoff lasted for a month before the crew eventually caved in and the ship was mothballed for four years.

THE END OF AN ERA

Despite interest from various potential bidders the *France* was eventually sold for $18 million (£10 million) to Knut Kloster of the Norwegian Caribbean Line in 1979. Having been rechristened the *Norway*, the ship was moved to the Lloyds shipyard in Bremerhaven for an $80-million refit. It was thought that an ocean liner with its deep draft, long, narrow shape and functional cabins would not find a niche in the cruise market but the *Norway* proved popular and was soon touring the Caribbean with thousands of passengers. Indeed, there was a scramble by other shipyards to build competitors.

The old lady was beginning to show her age, however. Poor maintenance saw several fires break out onboard, and she experienced many mechanical problems. She was also detained in a few ports for breaching safety regulations. Then a turbocharger fire in 1999 saw her sidelined in Barcelona for three weeks. Two years later she sailed out of New York Harbour on September 11, although her passengers wouldn't learn of the terrorist attacks until the following day.

The massive ships of the cruise industry were seen as potential terrorist targets and passenger numbers plummeted in the aftermath of the attacks. The *Norway* was immediately scheduled for retirement but her owners gambled on operating budget cruises from Miami instead. In 2003, one of her boilers exploded having been poorly maintained. The accident killed eight crewmen and injured 17, although no passengers were harmed. She then returned to Bremerhaven for repairs but was soon sold for scrap when she was found to contain huge amounts of asbestos. Because of the difficulty and danger associated with removing the substance, no country wanted to break her up. She was eventually scrapped off the coast of India and had all but disappeared by 2008.

The *QE2* and the *France/Norway* might have overseen the end of the era of great ocean liners, but they were also responsible for ushering in a new era of monstrous cruise ships where the ship itself was the destination. One ship refused to buckle to the pressure, however.

Centre: The
Costa Concordia
lies on her side.

LITTLE BOOK OF **LINERS**

The Last of the Few: *Queen Mary 2*

Cunard realized that there was still a market for trans-Atlantic travel so they commissioned naval architect Stephen Payne to submit designs for a new class of 84,000-tonne passenger liners in 1998. When the company heard about Carnival Cruise's plans for the 100,000-tonne *Destiny* class and Royal Caribbean's 140,000-tonne *Voyager* class, they revised their plans and decided to go for a single enormous liner of 150,000 tonnes so they could compete with the cruise lines. The result would be Cunard's latest super-liner, the *Queen Mary 2*, which would run alongside and eventually replace the aging *Queen Elizabeth 2*.

Harland & Wolff (Ireland), Aker Kværner (Norway), Fincantieri (Italy), Meyer Werft (Germany), and Chantiers de l'Atlantique (France) each bid for the building rights and the contract was signed with the French in November 2000 (in the same yard that had built Cunard's early rivals, the *Normandie* and the *France*).

The ship's keel was laid down in 2002 in Saint-Nazaire as hull number *G32*. More than 3,000 craftsmen and women then spent around eight million hours working on the ship (although at least 20,000 people were involved in the project as a whole). Around 300,000 pieces of steel were manufactured in blocks that were then assembled and welded together like a giant jigsaw in the dry dock.

Queen Mary 2 was launched in March

LITTLE BOOK OF **LINERS**

2003 and was then fitted out over the following six months. Her sea trials were conducted in late September and early November in the waters around Saint-Nazaire. An accident during the final stages of construction saw a gangway collapse into the dry dock and kill 16 workers who were showing their relatives around the new ship. Despite this setback, she was completed on time and on budget and *Queen Mary 2* was handed over to Cunard in Southampton on Boxing Day. Early in the New Year, Queen Elizabeth II named the ship after her grandmother.

Stephen Payne wanted the ship to include features borrowed from the great ocean liners of the past, notably *Queen Elizabeth 2* and the original *Queen Mary*. This included three thick black lines that wrapped around the edges of the bridge screen and at the aft end of the superstructure, both of which echoed the crossovers on the forward decks of the first *Queen Mary*.

Queen Mary 2 has 3.5 acres (1.5 hectares) of exterior deck space, five swimming pools, a Canyon Ranch Spa Club, a continuous wraparound promenade deck that passes behind the bridge and allows passengers to walk the ship's entire circumference, and a number of bars, restaurants and nightclubs.

For appearance and safety (waves in the North Atlantic regularly top 40 feet or 12 metres), the ship's lifeboats are

Centre: John McKenna's magnificent bronze sculpture of the ship.

82 feet (25 metres) from the waterline. Payne wanted to design the ship's stern profile in the old-fashioned spoon shape but the mounting of propeller pods meant needing a flat transom, so the builders reached a compromise of having a Constanzi stern (a combination of the two) which allowed for pod propulsion systems giving better seaworthiness, comfort and efficiency. *Queen Mary 2* also has a bulbous bow below the waterline to reduce drag and fuel consumption while increasing speed and range.

Her funnel is similar to that of *Queen Elizabeth 2*, although it is a slightly different shape because it would otherwise have been too high to pass under the Verrazano Narrows Bridge outside New York at high tide. As *Queen Mary 2* is too large to dock in many ports, passengers are ferried to and from the ship in her tenders at one of four loading stations (the tenders double as lifeboats in an emergency and are stored in davits alongside).

The ship is too big to fit through the Panama Canal and can only cross between the Atlantic and Pacific Oceans by rounding Cape Horn at the tip of South America or by crossing the Indian Ocean first. The decision not to limit her size was based on the fact that the *QE2* only passed through the canal once a year on her world cruise and that was deemed a bearable consequence of building the ship so large. Indeed, her increased capacity offset the extra fuel and time taken to round the cape and the fees for transiting the canal.

Many of the public rooms aboard *Queen Mary 2* are on the lower decks, while the passenger cabins are stacked above. Although not a traditional layout when comparing the *QM2* with her forebears, the new design allowed for larger rooms within a stronger hull, as well as for more of the passenger cabins to have private balconies with better views from higher up. This also meant that even large waves shouldn't affect the comfort and safety of the passengers.

Stephen Payne designed a central axis to the two main public room decks, like on the *Normandie*, but several smaller public rooms also span the width of the ship. The dining rooms were situated aft but not too close to the engine rooms or stern where vibration from the propellers is louder and the pitching more prominent, both of which could cause the passengers some discomfort.

The lowest passenger deck houses the

Illuminations Theatre, cinema, the first seaborne planetarium, the Royal Court Theatre, Grand Lobby, Empire Casino, Golden Lion Pub and the ground floor of the Britannia Restaurant. The deck above boasts the upper levels of the theatres and the Britannia Restaurant as well as a shopping mall, champagne bar, a wine bar, the Queen's Room, and one of the nightclubs. Deck 7 is also devoted to the public and contains the Canyon Ranch Spa, the Winter Garden, King's Court, and the Queen's Grill and Princess Grill restaurants. The public rooms on Deck 8 include an à la carte restaurant, an extensive library, a bookshop and the upper floor of the spa. There is also the large outdoor pool and terrace at the stern. There are kennels for 12 cats and dogs on starboard side aft but they are available only for trans-Atlantic crossings.

The King's Court is open all day and has a buffet restaurant serving breakfast and lunch. The space is divided up into separate sections that are decorated according to the theme of the dining areas that evening. The food is either Asian, a British-style carvery, Italian or you can also try the interactive Chef's Galley, where guests help prepare their own food.

Where you dine usually depends on your ticket. Most passengers travel on the Britannia fare and dine in the main restaurant but you can upgrade to a junior suite and eat in the Princess Grill or a full suite and dine in the Queen's Grill (the latter also has a private deck area with whirlpool that resemble the same areas on the *Queen Victoria* and the *Queen Elizabeth*). The remaining public areas can be used by all passengers.

The ship boasts more than 5,000 works of art (by 128 artists from 16 countries) in the main public rooms, corridors, staterooms and lobbies. Two of the most famous pieces are Barbara Broekman's *Tapestry*, which is an abstract of an ocean liner beneath the New York skyline that hangs in the Britannia Restaurant, and British sculptor John McKenna's bronze mural in the main lobby, a portrait of the ship that was inspired by the art deco mural in the original *Queen Mary*'s main dining room.

The *Queen Mary 2* is powered by four 16-cylinder Wärtsilä marine diesels generating 90,100 horsepower at 514rpm. She also has two General Electric gas turbines that provide a further 67,000 horsepower. This arrangement allows the ship to cruise economically

THE LAST OF THE FEW: QUEEN MARY 2

at low speed while also sustaining higher speeds at low revolutions. It is a layout that has been used by the navy for some time but *Queen Mary 2* is the first passenger ship to have it installed and indeed the first to feature gas turbines since a Finnish ferry in the late 1970s. The gas turbines are actually housed in soundproof chambers below the funnel rather than in the engine room because they require a constant supply of oxygen. Running pipes through the ship would have compromised on space and wasn't seriously considered.

Power is delivered to four Rolls-Royce pods with low-vibration propellers. The forward pair remain fixed but the aft pair can rotate so there was no need for the ship to be built with a rudder. The ship is the first quadruple screw passenger ship since the *France* in 1961 (*QM2* carries spare blades on her foredeck by the bridge screen in case the crew need to make repairs during a cruise).

In January 2004 *Queen Mary 2* set sail on her maiden voyage from Southampton to Fort Lauderdale in Florida with 2,620 passengers under the command of Captain Ronald Warwick (a previous commander of *Queen Elizabeth 2*). Warwick is the son of William Warwick who was also a senior Cunard captain who had taken charge of the *QE2*. The ship arrived back in Southampton a little late after her bow doors failed to shut while she was moored in Portugal.

Later that year she sailed to Athens to be used as a hotel during the Olympic Games. Guests included then Prime Minister Tony Blair and wife Cherie, French President Jacques Chirac, former US President George Bush and the American basketball team. Later passengers have included jazz musician Dave Brubeck, comedy legend John Cleese, actor Richard Dreyfuss, film director George Lucas, financier Donald Trump, and singers Carly Simon and Rod Stewart. The following year, the ship carried the first US-bound copy of JK Rowling's *Harry Potter and the Half-Blood Prince*, which was apparently the first time a book had been ferried to its launch aboard an ocean liner.

In January 2006 *Queen Mary 2* set sail on a circumnavigation of South America. While departing Fort Lauderdale, the ship clipped a wall and damaged one of her propeller pods which forced Commodore Warwick to amend the ship's itinerary because she couldn't make flank speed. This angered several

LITTLE BOOK OF **LINERS**

Right: *QM2's* bulbous bow improves performance. Note the three thruster openings immediately aft.

passengers and they staged a protest until Cunard agreed to refund their tickets. The ship was then forced to stop to make temporary repairs before she returned to Europe and a full repair in dry dock that summer. She was then back in dry dock later in the year to have the repaired propeller re-installed. The yard used this period to install sprinkler systems on all of the ship's balconies to comply with new safety regulations. Both bridge wings were extended by seven feet (two metres) to improve visibility.

Having completed her South American tour, *Queen Mary 2* met the original *Queen Mary* in Long Beach, California, where the latter is a hotel, tourist attraction and museum. Escorted by a flotilla of smaller ships, the Queens exchanged whistle salutes.

In January 2007, *Queen Mary 2* began her first world cruise. She eventually completed her circumnavigation in 81 days. In February, she met her ancestor, *Queen Elizabeth 2*, which was also on a world cruise, in Sydney Harbour. This was the first time two Cunard Queens had been seen together in Sydney since the original *Queen Mary* and *Queen Elizabeth* served as troop ships during the Second World War. Despite an early arrival time, the *Queen Mary 2*'s presence attracted so many viewers that the harbour bridge became blocked. The 1,600 passengers who disembarked in the city contributed an estimated US$3 million (£2.2 million) to the local economy.

Queen Mary 2 met the Cunard cruise ship *Queen Victoria* as well as the *QE2* in New York Harbour in 2008 for a celebratory fireworks display. The latter two ships had just crossed the Atlantic together and it marked the first time three Cunard Queens were in the same place at the same time.

Cunard believed this would be the only time the three great ships would be seen together (the *Queen Elizabeth 2* was due for retirement in late 2008) but they also met in Southampton that April. *Queen Mary 2* again met the *QE2* in Dubai in early 2009, after the latter's retirement. With *Queen Elizabeth 2*'s future uncertain, *Queen Mary 2* is the last ocean liner left in active service.

In January 2012, the *QM2* embarked on a three-month world cruise from Southampton to East Africa, Australia and Japan, before returning to Southampton via the Eurasian coastline and the Suez Canal.

Cruising & the Future

Where the magnificent liners of the past had transported millions of travellers, business people and immigrants across the world's oceans, the cruise ship tended to return tourists to the same port at the end of their holiday. The ship itself was part of the destination, its ports of call part of an itinerary designed to promote interest in various countries and their cultures.

There were more differences between the old liners and the new dedicated cruise ships too: liners tended to be long and sleek, but they had deep drafts and couldn't enter shallow ports. They also had enclosed weather decks to protect passengers from the cold and the wind and the rain so common on the trans-Atlantic run, although this was not suitable for cruising the tropics. Their cabins were designed around getting the highest number of people aboard and not having fewer people travelling in greater comfort. They were also built to withstand the odd rogue wave so had stronger hull plates and a higher freeboard.

The *QE2* and the *Norway* may have been partially converted into cruise ships but they were never designed as such. When the world stood up and took notice of the money that could be made from cruising, however, several lines took the plunge and ordered cruise ships to take them on. Such has been the swing away from the liners that, as we have

seen, there is now only one operating a full-time point-to-point service across the Atlantic: Cunard's *Queen Mary 2*.

The industry may have taken off in recent years but it had a slow start. Albert Ballin, then the general manager of Hamburg-America, designed the first dedicated cruise ship in the last few years of the 19th century. The *Prinzessin Victoria Luise* was completed in 1900 and was immediately dispatched to the North Atlantic. Aside from being one of the world's finest shipbuilders, Ballin was also a visionary. He realised that when passenger numbers dropped off during the winter, the line became less profitable. He remedied this by relocating the ship to the Caribbean for the winter where passengers could island hop in glorious weather while still enjoying the luxury of travelling by ocean liner. Cunard and White Star quickly followed suit and built ships that could be hastily transformed from cruise ship to liner and back depending on the season.

The jet aircraft slowly killed off the liners, although the *France* and the *QE2* just about held their own, and shipping for pleasure gradually declined. But these two great ships had shown the way forward and cruise lines began building more ships in the early 1980s to cater for a slow increase in demand. Royal Caribbean had been among the first to enter the market in 1968 and it was they who now took the lead.

Royal Caribbean

Founded by Norwegians Anders Wilhelmsen, I.M. Skaugen and Gotaas Larsen, the cruise line had its first ship, *Song of Norway*, in service after only two years. *Nordic Prince* and *Sun Viking* soon followed but it wasn't until the massive *Song of America* came into service in 1982 that the line got the recognition it deserved. The latter was then the third largest ship in the world after the *QE2* and *France*. The line concentrated on the Caribbean and soon had a good percentage of the market share around Haiti, Miami and the West Indies.

The company cleverly started buying up property in the Caribbean so its ships could call in and guests could enjoy the resorts as private destinations. The trend continued after the arrival of the *Sovereign of the Seas*, *Monarch of the Seas* and *Majesty of the Seas* in the late 1980s. To capitalise on a growing market share and general interest in the industry, the company was floated on the New York Stock Exchange in 1993. The revenue gained over the next two years allowed the company to move into new headquarters in Miami and replace the aging *Nordic Prince* with the *Legend of the Seas*.

Royal Caribbean showed more sound business sense by selling the older ships in their fleet and using the money to commission ever-larger vessels, like the 130,000-tonne *Voyager* class (although several smaller ships of the *Vision* class entered service first). They also bought Greek line Celebrity Cruises to increase their market share.

The turn of the new century saw Royal Caribbean introduce a number of new ships, from the *Navigator of the Seas* and *Brilliance of the Seas* to the *Mariner of the Seas* and *Jewel of the Seas*. Built in the Aker Finnyards in Turku, Finland, and launched in 2006, the *Freedom of the Seas* was then, at 1,112 feet (339 metres) and 154,407 tonnes, the largest passenger vessel in the world. The ship took cruising to a completely new level. She had 15 passenger decks, a vast central promenade with bars and restaurants, a water park, sports area, mini-golf course, skating rink and casino.

Such was the popularity of this enormous class of ships that Royal Caribbean decided to go even bigger with the *Oasis* class. Two ships, *Oasis of the Seas* and *Allure of the Seas*, were launched in 2009 and 2010 respectively and, incredibly, they were half as big again (in gross tonnage terms) as the *Freedom* class. At 1,181 feet (360 metres) and 225,000 tonnes, the ships could accommodate a maximum of 6,300 passengers and cruise at 23 knots (42km/h).

Twelve of their 22 ships are based in Europe, with several touring the Mediterranean, Baltic and North Seas. The company can now claim nearly a fifth of the world's cruising market.

Carnival Cruise Lines

Founded by Ted Arison in 1972, Carnival is now a joint British-American company based in Florida. Carnival decided not to compete directly with Royal Caribbean and instead concentrated on shorter trips with the emphasis on having fun onboard. The company decorated its first ships, *Empress of Canada* and *Mardi Gras*, in a lively Las Vegas-style and set about gathering a healthy market share by the end of the decade.

In 1978 the *Festivale* underwent a massive refurbishment programme and then, as their largest and fastest ship, took control of the lucrative Caribbean trade. Four years later the company introduced the *Tropicale*, then the newest and most technically advanced passenger ship in the world. Over the next decade Carnival reaped the benefits of the economic boom, which filtered down to the cruise industry and saw many competitors enter the market.

Three new ships, the 47,000-tonne *Holiday*, *Jubilee* and *Celebration*, earned the company the distinction of carrying the most passengers and becoming the most popular cruise line in the world. The directors also made the shrewd decision to float the company on the stock market to raise investment for more ships. Eight 70,000-tonne *Fantasy* class ships were the result, all of which entered service throughout the 1990s. In 1996 they also launched the largest cruise ship yet built, the 101,000-tonne *Carnival Destiny*. This move only highlighted the competition between themselves and Royal Caribbean but the real winners of this great rivalry were the passengers because each company was desperate to outdo one another in terms of luxury, service and price.

The end of the century saw Carnival introduce a new breed of cruise liners in the shape of the 102,000-tonne *Triumph* class, which included the ships *Carnival Triumph* and *Carnival Victory*. Carnival then introduced a further two classes of ship, the *Spirit* and *Conquest*. By the end of the decade, and despite the global economic downturn, interest in cruising was still high so the company introduced the 130,000-tonne *Carnival Dream*, *Carnival Magic* (the company's flagship) and *Carnival Breeze*.

Having taken over Princess Cruises and Holland-America (among others), the company now boasts the largest share of the market, its 23 ships accounting for more than 21 percent. This has led some to speculate that a 200,000-tonne *Pinnacle* class is just over the horizon.

Star Cruises

Founded by the Genting Group of Malaysia in 1993, Star Cruises is now the third largest company in the market and its 17 ships manage around a sixth of the world tourist trade. From an initial two cruise ferries, the company quickly expanded, preferring to buy up other lines and their ships as opposed to building vessels from new.

That changed in 1998 when the company took delivery of the *SuperStar Leo*, an 879-foot (268-metre), 75,000-tonne cruise liner, and the *SuperStar Virgo*, which, at 881 feet (269 metres), was a shade longer (although they displaced the same). The company then took control of Sun Cruises and set its sights on cornering the market in Asia and the Far East. In 2000, they consolidated their position by buying Orient Lines and the Norwegian Capricorn Line.

Since then, the company has bought and sold a number of ships (usually with the star sign theme in their name) and it remains the number one choice on the Orient.

MSC Cruises

Founded by Italian Achille Lauro in the 1960s, the company began life with two ships, both of which burned and then sank. The *Angelina Lauro* (formerly the Netherland Line's *Oranje*) had enjoyed 40 years of exemplary service (she was involved

Far Left: Carnival Cruise Lines' flagship, *Carnival Magic*.

in a collision with her running mate, *Willem Ruys*, in 1953 but it wasn't her fault), first as a hospital ship during the Second World War and then as a passenger liner. In 1964 both ships were sold to Lauro, with the latter becoming the *Achille Lauro*.

After her conversion from the *Oranje*, the *Angelina Lauro* gained 4,000 tonnes and 16 feet (five metres). In 1972 she was refitted again to bring her up to speed with the booming cruise market, but tragedy struck seven years later when a fire broke out onboard while she was berthed in the US Virgin Islands. The blaze raged for four days and effectively destroyed the beautiful ship. Her hulk was then transported across the Pacific to be scrapped but her hull had been so badly damaged in the fire that she took on water and eventually sank.

Her running mate also suffered from bad luck. In 1965 an explosion damaged her and she had to be extensively rebuilt. Like her sister, she was converted for the cruise industry in 1972 but promptly caught fire. She then collided with the cargo ship *Youseff*, which sank. Another fire in 1981 saw her laid up for more repairs.

In 1985 four men of the Palestinian Liberation Front seized the ship and demanded the release of 50 prisoners from Israeli jails. After two days the hijackers were convinced to abandon the ship and were arrested after their commercial flight was forced to land in Italy. Another explosion in the ship's engine room in 1994 sealed her fate and she sank off the coast of Somalia.

The following year, the company changed its name to MSC Cruises to distance itself from the problems. It then entered a period of great expansion, with four ships each from the *Mistral* and *Musica* classes being built in the first decade of the new century. Four giant *Fantasia* class ships now lead the line. They are approximately 140,000 tonnes each, 1,093 feet (333 metres) long and carry 5,300 passengers and crew in nearly 1,800 luxury staterooms.

MSC Divina cruises the Mediterranean at up to 24 knots (44km/h) and boasts an infinity pool, several upmarket lounges, a casino, Balinese massage parlour, a Formula 1 simulator and 4D cinema. It is surely one of the most remarkable ships ever built.

Louis Cruise Lines

L ouis Cruises is the fifth largest cruise line in the world and controls nearly 10 percent of the market share. Louis PLC is a subsidiary of a Cyprus-based travel and tourism group that was founded in 1935. In the early 1970s the company began chartering ferries for short cruises around Cyprus and they were so popular that they bought the small ship *MV Prinsessan* from Finnish company Birka Line in 1987. Having been rechristened *MV Princesa Marissa*, the line started operating cruises from Limassol to the Greek Islands, Egypt and Israel. By 1994, the company had bought three more ships to ply the profitable Eastern Mediterranean.

In the mid-90s Louis Cruise Lines began chartering ships such as the *Sapphire* to other companies like Thomson Cruises. In 1997, Thomson acquired the *Emerald* from Louis and this opened the door to competing charter companies like First Choice, who chartered the *Ausonia* in 1999.

By now the Louis fleet was rapidly expanding and they had eight of their own ships. They also bought a stake in the Greek Olympic Cruise Lines. Royal Olympic was already experiencing financial difficulty and the company eventually collapsed after the terrorist attacks in America in 2001.

In the first few years of the new millennium, Louis modernised their fleet by acquiring *Calypso* and then chartering *Nieuw Amsterdam* from the old Holland-America Line in 2003 (they then let her out to Thomson as the *Thomson Spirit*). Two years later Louis bought *Aquamarine* from Sun Cruises, which was also on the verge of bankruptcy. Their ship *Thomson Destiny* was then chartered from a Norwegian investment company and sub-chartered back to Thomson. Having expanded their fleet further, the company was in a position to sell its older ships, freeing up capital to engulf smaller lines that were still struggling in the global economic downturn (as they'd done with Royal Olympic Cruises, which morphed into Louis Hellenic Cruises with two of their former ships).

They expanded again in 2006 with the acquisition of the *Orient Queen* and *Sea Diamond* (a former Birka Line Baltic ferry) while *Calypso* was chartered to Thomson and the *Arielle* to Transocean. They also entered a franchise agreement with easyCruise to run tours throughout the Mediterranean In April 2007, the company took a massive hit when the *Sea Diamond* sank off the island of Santorini, however. Almost all of the passengers made it off in time but two people died and the negative publicity severely damaged the company's credibility.

Oceanic II and *Ruby* were seen as temporary replacements until *Cristal* and *Silja Opera* joined the fleet in 2007. The following year, the musical chairs continued: *Arielle* was returned to Transocean but she then reverted to her earlier name (*Aquamarine*) and rejoined Louis Hellenic Cruises. By 2008, however, this subsidiary brand was being phased out. The line continued its recovery with the acquisition of the *Norwegian Dream* from Star Cruises, in a deal that was supposed to be the first of many, but in late 2008 Louis cancelled the *Norwegian Dream* due to concerns over its seaworthiness.

In 2009, the company shortened its name to Louis Cruises and bought *Thomson Destiny* and *Thomson Spirit* that had previously been under charter. The *Princesa Marissa* and *Serenade* were then sold for scrap. With the loss of two more ships the following year, the company was down to a fleet of just five but 2012 saw a revival in fortunes. Louis signed a new agreement with Thomson and the *Louis Majesty* replaced the aging *Thomson Destiny*. The latter was recalled for an extensive refit and returned to the Louis fleet as *Louis Olympia* in late 2012 for sailings from Piraeus to the Greek Islands. The *Sapphire* was then sold for scrap.

Disney Cruises

The Disney brand entered the cruise industry in 1995 with the commissioning of two 964-foot (293-metre), 83,000-tonne ships: the *Disney Magic*, which entered service in 1998; and the *Disney Wonder*, which sailed the following year. The ships toured the Bahamas, Caribbean

Far Left: The *Louis Majesty.*

and the Mexican Riviera, as well as Europe, the Pacific Northwest of America and Alaska with up to 2,400 passengers and 1,000 crew.

In 2011 and 2012 they were joined respectively by the *Disney Dream* and the *Disney Fantasy*, 1,115-foot (340-metre), 128,000-tonne giants to rival the Carnival and Royal Caribbean ships. Both were designed and built from the keel up to be family-friendly so they have no casinos and fewer bars and nightclubs. Their shows and restaurants are themed around the Disney brand and have won many international awards. A crew of 1,438 caters for around 4,000 passengers.

Disney Dream features a 765-foot (233-metre) waterslide that winds down over four decks and even extends 13 feet (four metres) over the ship's side. It also has digital sports simulators, walking tracks and a mini-golf course, and a 24-foot (seven-metre) TV screen attached to the forward funnel. All Disney ships are based in Port Canaveral in Florida. The company can only claim around three percent of the world cruise market but two more *Dream* class ships are rumoured to be in the pipeline.

Right: P&O's *Oriana.*

P&O

The P&O Cruise Line originated in 1822 with the founding of the Peninsular & Oriental Steam Navigation Company. This entity began as a partnership between ship broker Brodie Wilcox and sailor Arthur Anderson, and they soon started a fledgling line between England and Spain/Portugal (hence the 'Peninsular' part of their title).

Fifteen years later the two men won a contract to deliver mail to the same region via *RMS Don Juan*. The ship collected mail from Cornwall before setting sail. The outward journey passed without a hitch but the ship struck rocks on the homeward leg. Thankfully all the mail was salvaged and the company survived its first major scare.

In 1840, the company secured another contract to deliver mail to Gibraltar, Malta and Egypt, which is when the 'Oriental' was added to their title. However, with no ships available for the route, they had no option but to merge with Liverpool's Trans-Atlantic

Steamship Company. This gave them the use of two ships: the 1,300-tonne *Great Liverpool* and the brand new 1,600-tonne *Oriental*.

In 1844 P&O introduced a passenger service to the same destinations from Southampton but they added Athens and the Greek Islands as ports of call. In effect, this marked the beginning of the tourist cruise industry as we know it today, and P&O are rightly considered the world's first cruise line. The company then trialled round trips to Istanbul (then Constantinople) and Alexandria and was soon enjoying a boom in trade. Their ships gradually grew larger and more luxurious as passengers clamoured for the glamour. By the end of the century, the company was running all-steel ships like the *Ravenna*, and the first ship with electric lighting in 1889, the *Valetta*.

At the dawn of the new century, P&O introduced a class system on its 6,000-tonne *Vectis* (the ship could carry 150 first-class passengers). Just before the outbreak of war in 1914, the company made further gains and expanded its fleet to nearly 200 ships by merging with the British India Steam Navigation Company, although more than a hundred of these were commandeered for war service. Where the war had been unkind to Cunard, White Star and NDL, it was relatively easy on P&O and the company only lost 17 ships (although another 70 were lost by its subsidiaries).

At the end of the war, P&O was therefore in a strong financial position and the company was able to buy a controlling share in the Orient Steam Navigation Company, which opened up the lucrative mail route to Australia and the Far East. The money rolled in and P&O were able to expand again, taking delivery of another 20 passenger ships. By 1925, the company was ready to restart its cruise itinerary and it was soon operating its first turbo-electric ship, *Viceroy of India*.

The company didn't come off as well after the Second World War. It lost nearly 160 ships, including the liners *Viceroy of India*, *Cathay*, *Oronsay* and *Orcades*. The company was dealt a further blow when the airlines began to steal trade on their most popular routes. The only way to counter the threat was to build bigger, faster and more luxurious ships. Innovations in design and propulsion soon cut the sailing time to Australia to a month. Although no one knew it at the time, in 1955 P&O ordered their last passenger liners: *Canberra* and *Oriana*. These two modern giants topped 30 knots (56km/h) and chopped another week off the sailing time.

In 1961, P&O bought the rest of the Orient Line and renamed its passenger service P&O-Orient. It was seen as a last desperate move to counter the aviation threat and to attract customers drifting away from the traditional trans-Atlantic liner run. With the oil crisis biting, the company restructured and divided into several separate organisations, one of which was a passenger division with 13 ships. Many of their outdated ships were now sold for scrap to raise capital and they bought Princess Cruises with the revenue in 1974.

Three years later P&O re-branded again and divided into P&O Cruises and P&O Cruises Australia. In 1979 the *Kungsholm* was bought and given an extensive refit before being renamed *Sea Princess*. She was soon replaced by the *Oriana* in Australia, however, so *Sea Princess* returned to the UK. When the *Canberra* returned from the Falklands, she took over from *Sea Princess*. But the *Canberra*'s days were numbered so, in 1995, P&O reacted by ordering its first new ship for the British market, the *Oriana*. This meant that *Canberra* could be scrapped in 1997.

At the dawn of the new millennium, *Arcadia* became the first P&O ship to be adults only, a trend that continued with the *Adonia*. In 2000 *Aurora* and *Oceana* also joined P&O. Another former Princess Lines ship, *Artemis*, was added in 2005 (although she herself was replaced in 2011 by the former *Royal Princess* and renamed). At only 30,000 tonnes, she is the smallest ship in P&O's fleet. This fleet will be expanded again in 2015 with the addition of a 141,000-tonne cruise ship.

Centre: The world's largest cruise ship, Royal Caribbean's *Oasis of the Seas.*

ALSO AVAILABLE IN THE LITTLE BOOK SERIES

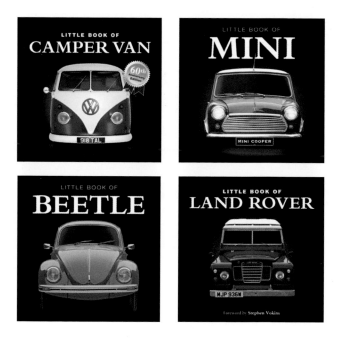

ALSO AVAILABLE IN THE LITTLE BOOK SERIES

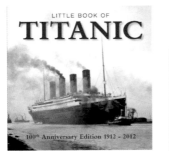

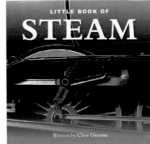

The pictures in this book were provided courtesy of the following:

WIKIMEDIA COMMONS

Design & Artwork: SCOTT GIARNESE

Published by: DEMAND MEDIA LIMITED & G2 ENTERTAINMENT LIMITED

Publishers: JASON FENWICK & JULES GAMMOND

Written by: LIAM MCCANN